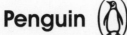 **Penguin**  **Readers**

PRIVATE

JAMES PATTERSON
AND MAXINE PAETRO

LEVEL

RETOLD BY NICK BULLARD

ILLUSTRATED BY KEVIN HOPGOOD

SERIES EDITOR: SORREL PITTS

PENGUIN BOOKS

UK | USA | Canada | Ireland | Australia
India | New Zealand | South Africa

Penguin Books is part of the Penguin Random House group of companies
whose addresses can be found at global.penguinrandomhouse.com.
www.penguin.co.uk www.puffin.co.uk www.ladybird.co.uk

Private first published by Century, 2010
This Penguin Readers edition published by Penguin Books Ltd 2019

001

Original text written by James Patterson and Maxine Paetro
Text for Penguin Readers edition adapted by Nick Bullard
Text copyright © James Patterson, 2010
Illustrated by Kevin Hopgood
Illustrations copyright © Penguin Books Ltd, 2019
Cover (City of Los Angeles at night) © logoboom/shutterstock.com;
(Futuristic Urban City) © EpicStockMedia/shutterstock.com

Printed in and bound in Great Britain by Clays Ltd, Elcograf S.p.A.

A CIP catalogue record for this book is available from the British Library

ISBN: 978–0–241–39770–1

All correspondence to
Penguin Books
Penguin Random House Children's Books
80 Strand, London WC2R 0RL

Contents

People in the story

Jack

Andy

Justine

Emilio

Sci

Mo-bot

Rudolph Crocker

Scylla

New words

blood

earring

gun

necklace

text messages

van

Note about the story

James Patterson is an American writer, and his books have sold more than 385 million copies around the world. Maxine Paetro has written more than twenty books with James Patterson. In *Private*, they tell a story about Jack Morgan and the work of his **company***. Jack's company, Private, helps people and the police around the city of Los Angeles.

Before-reading questions

1 Look at the cover of the book, and then look quickly at the pictures inside. Which sentences are true? Write your answers in your notebook.

   a Some people die in this story.

   b This story is about animals.

   c This story happened a long time ago.

   d Some of the people in this story work for the police.

2 The story happens in and around Los Angeles. Which sentences about the city are true?

   a Most people in Los Angeles travel by bicycle.

   b Los Angeles is near the ocean.

   c Los Angeles is a modern city.

   d Los Angeles is very cold.

*Definitions of words in **bold** can be found in the glossary on pages 62–63.

CHAPTER ONE

At the Golden Globes

Jack Morgan got out of his dark blue Lamborghini near the Beverly Hilton. It was the night of the Golden Globes, and he was with a beautiful and famous **movie star**. He helped Guinevere Scott-Evans out of the car, and she held his hand hard. Guinevere **trusted** Jack, and she trusted his **company**, Private. Everyone trusted Private; it was the best.

But then Jack's oldest friend, Andy Cushman, **called** him.

Andy spoke quickly. "Jack, come to my house now! I need you."

"It's not a good time. What's wrong?" asked Jack.

"It's Shelby. She's **dead**," said Andy. Shelby and Andy married six months **ago**.

Guinevere wasn't happy, but Jack took her to

her table. Then, he was on the road to Andy's house in Bluffs. He stopped near the open front door, took out his **gun**, and went in.

"Andy?" shouted Jack.

"Jack! I'm in the bedroom."

Jack went through the house, his gun in his hand. In the bedroom, there were clothes everywhere. Shelby was on the bed, with **blood** on her head.

"What happened?" asked Jack.

Andy was near Shelby, his head in his hands. "Someone **shot** her. Please find him!"

Jack took photos of everything in the room. "Did you call the police?" he asked.

"No, I wanted you here," said Andy.

"Do you have a gun?" asked Jack.

"No," said Andy.

"OK, you must understand. The police will want to talk to you. They always want it to be easy. They will think, 'A woman is dead—did her husband kill her?' But I can help," said Jack.

He called the police and waited for them to arrive.

CHAPTER TWO

A young woman dies

Justine worked with Jack at Private. People trusted her, too. Tonight, she was in an expensive Italian restaurant. Then, the **chief of police** called her.

"**Another** young woman is dead," Justine told her friend. "I must go."

In two years, eleven young women in Los Angeles were dead. Now, it was twelve. The killer always took something from the women—hair, a **necklace**, clothes. Then, the killer emailed the chief of police and told him about the women's things. Nobody knew where the emails came from, but the emails all had the same name—*Steemcleena*. The police found the women's things, but they couldn't find Steemcleena. The police wanted Justine, and Private, to help them find the killer.

Emilio Cruz, from Private, stopped his Mercedes at the restaurant door, and Justine got in. "What do you know about this girl?" asked Justine.

"Her name is Connie Yu. She was sixteen and very intelligent," said Emilio. "She was on the ground behind a restaurant. There was an **earring** in her left ear. There was no right ear."

Emilio stopped in a small, dark street near some police cars. They walked past the police and spoke to the doctor.

"We'll get an email about the ear in a day or two," Emilio said.

At 2 a.m., Justine and Emilio were at Private's offices. They talked to Sci, Private's **forensic expert**. "We have the woman's bag and cell phone," said Justine. "Can you look for **DNA** on them?"

"Of course," said Sci. "I can work all night on it."

CHAPTER THREE

At Private

The next morning, Justine, Emilio, Sci, and Mo-bot, the computer expert, were in the office.

Jack opened his laptop and showed them the photos from Andy's bedroom. "Look at these," he said. "I can't see anything important. Can you?"

"Did the killer take anything from the house?" asked Justine.

"No, he took nothing," said Jack.

"And were Andy and Shelby happy together?" asked Emilio.

"Yes," said Jack. "Very happy."

"OK," said Justine. "This killer is a **professional**. But why did he kill Shelby?"

"The police always like easy answers. They will

think one thing: Andy killed her," said Emilio. "Did Andy kill her?"

"No, he didn't," said Jack. "I know Andy well. He loved Shelby."

"What next?" asked Mo-bot.

"We look at Andy and Shelby," said Jack. "We talk to their friends and to people they work with. Let's go."

"Wait!" said Justine. "I have some news on the young woman. We have her bag. Sci couldn't find any new DNA, but Mo-bot looked at her phone."

"I looked at the **text messages**," said Mo-bot. "There were hundreds, from twenty or thirty people. I looked at the numbers, and they are all friends or family. But there is one strange message—I can't get the number for it. Look!"

A text message came up on the wall.

```
Connie. It's Linda. My mom took my
phone. I must talk to you. Can we
meet? Please! Behind the restaurant.
At 8.30 p.m. Don't tell anyone.
```

"I talked to Linda," said Mo-bot. "Her mother didn't take her phone. Linda didn't send that message. The killer got into Connie's phone and found all her friends. Then, he sent her that message from his phone."

"But we can't find the number of the killer's phone," said Sci. "It isn't possible."

"Who is Steemcleena?" asked Jack.

———

Rudolph Crocker left his office at 7 p.m. and went for a drink. At 9 p.m., he was at home and ready for a run. He ran out to Marina del Rey and thought about Connie Yu. That was a great evening.

There was nobody near him. He stopped near a boat and put something on it. Then, he went home and sent an email to the Chief of Police.

You can find Connie Yu's ear on a boat in Marina del Rey. Steemcleena

CHAPTER FOUR

Another young woman

Jason Pilser got a text message at work at 3 p.m.

```
Scylla, your big night is Saturday.
Be ready. Steemcleena
```

"Scylla" was Jason's computer name. At 6 p.m., he left his office and drove to a store. He bought some **gloves** and some **electric cable**. He didn't pay with a card, and he looked down at the ground. He didn't want the cameras in the store to see him.

The big night was in three days. He was ready to kill his first woman.

———————

"I'm going for a walk!" Marguerite Esperanza shouted to her grandmother. It was Saturday evening. Marguerite walked out the house and on to Rowena Avenue. A text message came on to her phone.

`Hi Marg. It's Lamar. Where are you?`

She read it and answered.

`I'm on Rowena.`

Lamar was a really nice boy. Marguerite liked him.

`Do you want to get a pizza?` asked Lamar.

`OK`, Marguerite answered.

Marguerite called her grandmother. "I'm getting a pizza with Lamar," she said. "And he'll walk home with me. Is that OK?"

The black **van** was near Rowena Avenue. The driver was Steemcleena. Scylla and Morbid were in the back of the van.

"She's out of her house," said Morbid. He gave the laptop to Scylla.

Scylla wrote a message: `Hi Marg. It's Lamar. . .`

Marguerite answered. Scylla wrote another message. The van stopped near the pizza restaurant and waited. Then, they saw Marguerite in the street.

"Go!" shouted Morbid. Scylla got out of the van. He pulled a bag over Marguerite's head from behind, and he and Morbid **threw** her into the van. Steemcleena drove away quickly.

"Help!" shouted Marguerite.

"Be quiet!" shouted Morbid. "Maybe you can **win** the game."

"Win?" asked Marguerite. "What do you mean?"

Steemcleena stopped the van in a park, with nobody near. Morbid and Steemcleena were behind Scylla. This was Scylla's game.

Marguerite got out of the van quickly, and she pulled the bag off her head. She couldn't run away; Steemcleena and Morbid could stop her. But she was tall and strong, and ready for Scylla. Her hand flew out and hit him on the nose.

There was blood on Scylla's face now, and he was angry. He ran at her, but she kicked him hard in the stomach. And then she kicked him again.

Steemcleena looked at Morbid. "She's too good for Scylla," he said. He took out a gun and shot Marguerite in the head. Then, Scylla put on the gloves and put the cable around the dead woman's **neck**. He took her shoes and put them in the van.

"That wasn't good," said Steemcleena to Scylla. "But maybe you'll win the next game."

CHAPTER FIVE

Scylla's next game

Justine met Police Lieutenant Nora Cronin in the park at 4 a.m. on Sunday. "The Chief of Police is here," said Nora. "He wants to talk to you."

The Chief was with three police **officers** near Marguerite's body. Justine walked up to him.

"It's good to see you," he said. "We need your help. Thirteen women are dead. And look! Somebody shot her dead—so why is there cable around her neck?"

"It's very strange," said Justine. "And where's her handbag?"

"There's no handbag," said the Chief, "and no shoes. I'm waiting for the email."

———

On Sunday evening, Scylla was on the **terrace** of his apartment, at the top of a tall building. The city was beautiful at night, but he didn't look at it. His face and body were black and blue. "That girl was strong," he thought. Then, he read the message from Morbid again.

```
You weren't good yesterday, Scylla.
Steemcleena isn't happy. But you can
play again tonight. We have someone
for you. Be ready at 7 p.m.
```

Morbid and Steemcleena were at the door now, and Scylla went to open it.

"How's the nose?" asked Morbid.

"OK," said Scylla. "Do you want a drink?"

"No," said Steemcleena. "Let's go on the terrace. I want to show you something."

The three men walked on to the terrace and looked down at the city. Then, Steemcleena turned to Scylla. "You think you can play again?" he asked. "You can. But you're playing with us."

Steemcleena took Scylla's legs, and Morbid took his arms, and they threw him over the terrace wall.

———————

Justine and Jack were at Private with Mo-bot. They talked about Marguerite.

"The killer sent an email," said Justine, "and we found her shoes. Sci is looking at them now, but they're probably clean."

"The killer is using a van to look for the young women, I think," said Mo-bot. "He has a laptop and a radio in the van, and he can send messages to the women's cell phones. He can stop messages to their phones from other people, too. And maybe he can find them in the street from their phones."

"Is that possible?" asked Jack.

"I don't know. I'll ask Sci about it," said Mo-bot. "His friend Kit-Kat knows about cell phones."

"I remembered something important," said Justine. "Someone killed a woman about five years ago in the same street as Connie Yu. Her name was Wendy Borman. The killer took her phone. And her necklace."

"Five years ago!" said Jack. "Maybe it's not thirteen women. Maybe it's more! We have work to do!"

An angry husband can kill

On Monday morning, Andy was at Private. Jack had something to tell him.

"I can't sleep," Andy said. "I think about Shelby all the time."

"Andy," said Jack. "We talked to a lot of people about Shelby. She had a lot of friends—you know that. And we found one very good friend. The movie star Bob Santangelo. She saw him every week."

"That's not true!" shouted Andy. "She loved me."

"Maybe she loved you," said Jack. "But she loved Santangelo, too. Did you know that?"

"No, I didn't!" shouted Andy. "It's not true!"

Andy left. Jack and Sci talked about Santangelo.

"Did Andy know about Santangelo?" asked Sci.

"I don't know," said Jack.

"An angry husband can kill, you know," said Sci.

"I know, Sci," said Jack. "But Andy's a good man, and he's my friend. He didn't kill Shelby."

"I understand. You don't want to hear it," said Sci. "But maybe he did."

Justine was at the police station with Lieutenant Nora Cronin.

"I looked on the internet," said Justine, "but can you tell me more about Wendy Borman?"

"One thing isn't on the internet," said Nora. "An eleven-year-old girl called Christine Castiglia saw something. She and her mother were in a coffee shop on Melrose Avenue. Christine saw two boys push Wendy into a van. Her mother didn't see anything, and Christine didn't see a lot. The boys were white. One had a long nose and big ears; the other had long hair."

"But Christine is sixteen now," said Justine. "We need to talk to her again."

CHAPTER SEVEN

Help from Sci's friends

Sci lived in an apartment with a lot of computers. On Monday evening, he sat at a computer and talked to his friend Kit-Kat in Sweden.

"You asked about cell phones," said Kit-Kat. "I can help. Someone in the United States of America has a new **program**. It can find a phone and get inside it. Then, it can send messages from the phone. And nobody knows it is happening."

"That's great, Kit-Kat," said Sci. "Do you know who made this program?"

"His name is Morbid. He's American, I think."

"Thanks, Kit-Kat. You're wonderful!"

Then, Sci sent a message to his friend Darren, who was in India. Darren played games on computers.

```
Do you know a player called Morbid?

Yes. I saw a message from a player
called Scylla about Morbid. On
Saturday.

What did he say?

He said: "I'm playing a new game with
Morbid." Then, there was a message
from Morbid the next day. "Scylla can
fly. He flew off his terrace. Flying
is easy, but the streets are hard."
```

Sci looked on the internet. On Sunday, a man **fell**

off a terrace in Los Angeles and died. His name was Jason Pilser. "Was that Scylla?" Sci thought.

Sci met Jack in a coffee shop early on Tuesday morning.

"Jack, I have some news. Lots of people like playing games on the internet. In some of these games you kill people, but you're playing—it's a game. I think some men in Los Angeles are playing a game, but they are really killing people. Not on the computer, but on the streets."

33

"Who are these men?" asked Jack.

"One man is—was—Jason Pilser. His computer name was Scylla. Another man is Morbid. Scylla died on Sunday night. The police say he fell off his terrace. But maybe someone pushed him."

"Let's go to his apartment," said Jack.

Jack and Sci met Nora at the apartment building, and they went up together. There wasn't anything interesting in the living room. But in the bedroom were a laptop and a cell phone.

"I'll take the computer back to Mo-bot," said Sci. "But I'll look at the phone now." He started to read the text messages.

"Jack, look at this." Sci gave the phone to Jack.

```
It's tonight, Scylla. You're the
killer. Steemcleena
```

"It's from Steemcleena!" said Jack. "He's working in a group!"

CHAPTER EIGHT

They're going to kill again

Justine took the police photos of Wendy Borman's body to the office at Private. She also took a bag of Wendy's clothes. "Sci can look at those," she thought. "There may be DNA on them!"

Justine looked at the photos of Wendy, dead, behind the restaurant. Five years ago, the police found Wendy's bag next to her, but her necklace was not there. Wendy always wore the necklace, and Justine found a photo of it. It had a **star** on it.

Then, she went to find Christine Castiglia in school.

Justine found Christine in the school restaurant. "Do you remember Wendy Borman?" she asked.

"I was only eleven," said Christine.

"Yes, but can you remember anything? What did you see?" asked Justine.

"A van stopped, and two boys got out and pushed a girl into the back. Then, they drove away. It was very quick," said Christine.

"And you saw the driver?" said Justine.

"He had a long nose. And big ears," said Christine.

"And the van?" said Justine.

"It was black. I remember a word on it: Gateway," said Christine.

Gateway. This was new. Gateway was an expensive school in Santa Monica.

"Thank you, Christine," said Justine.

Sci worked for hours on Wendy Borman's clothes. He looked for DNA and he found it—from two different men. "Yes!" he said.

He heard someone at the door, and Mo-bot ran into his office. "Sci, they are going to kill again. This week! I looked at Jason's computer. There were thousands of messages, and I read them all. Look at this one!"

```
Morbid, Scylla. Here's the next
woman. She lives in Silver Lake, and
her name is Graciella. Steemcleena
```

There was a photo of a young woman.

"I'll call Jack," said Sci.

CHAPTER NINE

Help from Carmine Noccia

On Tuesday afternoon, Jack was in his office with Emilio. They knew something about the young women's killers now, but nothing about Shelby's.

"Andy isn't a killer," Jack said. "Shelby's killer was a professional. There was no DNA, no gun, nothing. We need to talk to Carmine Noccia in Las Vegas."

Carmine and his family knew every professional killer from California to Florida. Jack didn't often work with men like Carmine. But, once, Carmine asked for Private's help—his daughter ran away, and he wanted her back. Jack found her. Carmine never forgot a friend.

"We'll fly to Las Vegas," Jack said.

Carmine was very rich, and his home was in a park, half an hour from the airport. Two big men came to meet Jack and Emilio at the door and took their guns from them.

Carmine was in the sitting room.

"Good to see you, Jack," said Carmine.

"I need your help," said Jack.

"Jack, you helped me, and I'll help you. But don't ask again," said Carmine.

"Someone killed my friend Shelby Cushman in Los Angeles—a professional. Who was the killer, do you know?" said Jack.

"I don't know. But I can ask. I'll call you when I know," said Carmine.

The **call** from Carmine came late at night. He only said two words: "Bo Montgomery."

Jack called Emilio early Wednesday morning. Emilio said he knew Bo Montgomery. Bo was a professional killer, and he lived on a horse farm in the Agoura Hills.

Jack and Emilio drove there fast. They stopped near the farmhouse.

A door opened slowly, and a man came out. He had a big dog, and in his arms was an AK-47. "What do you want?" he asked.

"I'm Jack Morgan, from Private. I'm working for Andy Cushman. Someone killed his wife, Shelby. Who paid for that?"

Bo Montgomery thought for a minute and then spoke slowly. "I don't know Shelby Cushman. I don't know any women in Bluffs."

Then, he wrote a name on the ground with the end of his gun. Jack looked at the name, and then Bo kicked it away.

"Goodbye, Mr Morgan," he said. "And please, drive slowly. The horses get frightened."

CHAPTER TEN
DNA

Christine Castiglia wanted to meet Justine again, on Wednesday after school.

"Let's go to the coffee shop on Melrose Avenue," said Christine. "I'll remember better there about the boys and the van."

"Great," said Justine.

The coffee shop was the same as five years before. "My mum and I sat here," said Christine. She went to a table near the window.

Justine had yearbooks for three years from Gateway school with photos of all the students. She put them on the table. "Can you look at these? Maybe one of the boys is there."

Christine turned the pages of the yearbooks. She stopped and looked at a photo of a group of boys. "That's him!" she said. She showed Justine. The boy had a long nose and big ears.

Justine looked at the name under the photo. Rudolph Crocker.

"Great job, Christine!" she said.

She opened her laptop and looked for Rudolph Crocker. There were two in Los Angeles. The first was sixty-six years old. The second worked for a small company on Wilshire Boulevard. And there was a photo of him. It was the boy, five years older.

Now, Justine needed his DNA.

Justine went to see Nora Cronin at the police station. "We have DNA from Wendy Borman's clothes," she told her. "It's from two men, but we don't know them. But I talked to Christine Castiglia. We looked at some photos, and she saw this boy. He pushed Wendy Borman into the van. Look!" She showed Nora a photo on her computer. "His name is Rudolph Crocker. He's twenty-three now, and he lives and works in Los Angeles."

"Maybe this is Steemcleena. And you want his DNA?" said Nora.

"Yes. Can you help me?" said Justine.

———

Nora and Justine stopped their car near Crocker's apartment building. They watched and waited. Crocker left the apartment at 6 p.m. and went for a run. He came home, and at 8 p.m. he came out and got into a new, dark blue Toyota van. He drove to a **bar** called Whiskey Blue and went in.

The two women went into the bar after him.

There were a lot of people in the bar. Crocker was in the corner with a man with long hair. Justine bought drinks, and the two women watched.

Half an hour later, the men finished their drinks and left. Nora and Justine quickly went to the men's table and took the glasses.

In the car, Justine called Sci. "Can you meet us at Private in twenty minutes?" she asked. "We have some DNA for you!"

Late on Wednesday, Jack and Emilio drove back to the city from the Agoura Hills. Jack left Emilio at his apartment and went to see Andy Cushman.

"Jack, why are you here now? It's 1 a.m. You look tired!" said Andy.

"I am tired," said Jack. "Today, I drove to the

Agoura Hills. How much did you pay Bo Montgomery to kill Shelby?"

Andy started to cry. "You don't understand, Jack," he said. "She was with another man, that movie star. I couldn't live with that!"

Jack didn't speak. He hit Andy in the face, three times, and left.

CHAPTER ELEVEN

A dark blue van

The next morning, Sci had news for Justine and Nora about the DNA.

"I have DNA from one of the glasses," he said. "Not Crocker's glass, the other man's. It's the same as the DNA on Wendy Borman's clothes."

"Who is this other man?" asked Justine. "We don't know him. Is it Morbid?"

"Maybe. And what did you get from Crocker's glass?" Nora asked Sci.

"I couldn't get DNA from Crocker's glass. It was too dirty," said Sci.

Justine looked at Nora. "What now?" she asked.

"We must find Crocker!" said Nora.

Mo-bot worked all morning on her computer, and then she found something. She called Jack.

"Morbid wants to kill Graciella tonight! He's sending her text messages from a friend, Lulu. Graciella is answering these messages from Lulu. She says, 'See you after school', but I don't know where they are meeting."

"Where is Morbid?" asked Jack.

"I don't know," said Mo-bot.

Justine and Nora drove to Crocker's office on Wilshire Boulevard.

"Mr. Crocker is on vacation today," said the woman at the desk.

They drove fast to his apartment, but he wasn't there.

"Let's find his van!" said Nora.

Nora called the police station. "We're looking for a new, dark blue Toyota van. Every police car must look for it."

Then, she and Justine waited in their car near Crocker's apartment building.

The call came back to Nora. "The dark blue van is in Silver Lake. It was on Alvarado Street, but we can't find it now."

"We must stop that van!" shouted Nora into the radio. "The driver is a killer!"

Jack and Emilio were on the road, too. Mo-bot called Jack.

"I'm reading more messages from Morbid to Graciella," she told him. "She's in Glendale, and he wants to meet at Ralph's Supermarket."

Graciella was in the street near the supermarket. Morbid walked up to her.

"Graciella?" he said. "I'm a friend of Lulu's. She's in hospital. Can you come with me to visit her? She wants to see you."

Morbid put his hand on Graciella's arm. Jack ran across the street and hit him in the stomach.

Morbid fell down, and Jack held him. "Where's Rudolph Crocker?" shouted Jack.

Nora and Justine got to Glendale quickly, too. Crocker's van was behind the supermarket, with a police car next to it. Nora talked to a police officer.

"Crocker is in the van, Lieutenant," he said. "He won't open the doors."

Justine walked up to the van. Crocker was sitting with his hands on his head. "Get out of the van, Crocker," she said. He smiled at her.

Justine hit the van window hard with her gun. She put her hand into the van, opened the door, and pulled Crocker out. There was blood and glass everywhere.

At the supermarket, the police took Morbid away. Jack and Emilio walked to Crocker's van. They found Justine with her foot on Crocker's back.

"Are you OK?" asked Jack. "There's a lot of blood on you."

"It's not mine," said Justine. "It's Crocker's."

Jack put some glass with blood on it in a bag and gave it to Emilio. "Get this to Sci," he said. "There's DNA here."

The police took Crocker away. Justine looked at Nora. "We need to go to his apartment and look for Wendy Borman's necklace."

Justine and Nora looked everywhere in Crocker's apartment. They found nothing. Justine opened the closet in the bedroom to look at Crocker's clothes again. The light was on a **string**, and she pulled it. She looked at the end of the string in her hand. It was the star from Wendy's necklace.

"We've caught them, Justine," said Jack, back at Private. "Sci looked at the DNA from Crocker's blood. It's the same as the DNA from Wendy's clothes."

The next morning, Jack's phone woke him early.

"Jack, it's Carmine Noccia. I have some bad news

for you. Your friend Andy Cushman is dead. His car went off the road near Marin, and it went into the ocean."

"Did anybody see Andy's car go into the ocean?" said Jack.

"Oh, yes. One of my cousins saw it. He was the only person there. Have a good day," said Carmine.

Jack looked at his phone for a minute and thought, "Carmine's cousin killed Andy." Then, he turned and threw it out of the window. It was time for a new phone and a new phone number.

During-reading questions

Write the answers to these questions in your notebook.

CHAPTER ONE

1 Where is Jack at the beginning of the story?
2 Who calls Jack?
3 Why does this person call Jack?

CHAPTER TWO

1 How many young women are now dead?
2 How old was Connie Yu?

CHAPTER THREE

1 Does the killer take anything from Andy's house?
2 Who sends Connie Yu a strange message?
3 Where does Rudolph Crocker put Connie Yu's ear?

CHAPTER FOUR

1 What does Jason buy at the store?
2 What does Scylla pull over Marguerite's head?
3 After the men throw Marguerite into the van, where does Steemcleena stop the van?

CHAPTER FIVE

1 When does Justine meet Nora Cronin at the park?
2 Where do Steemcleena and Morbid throw Scylla?

CHAPTER SIX

1 What is the name of Shelby's movie-star friend?
2 Who helps Justine at the police station?

CHAPTER SEVEN

1 Who lives in an apartment with a lot of computers?
2 When does Sci meet Jack in a coffee shop?

CHAPTER EIGHT

1 Where does Justine find Christine Castiglia?
2 What word is on the black van?

CHAPTER NINE

1 Where does Carmine Noccia live?
2 Where does Bo Montgomery live?

CHAPTER TEN

1 Where does Christine see a picture of Rudolph Crocker?
2 Where does Rudolph Crocker go at 8 p.m.?

CHAPTER ELEVEN

1 Why can't Sci get DNA from Crocker's glass?
2 Andy's car went off the road. Where did it go?

After-reading questions

1 What is Sci's job?
2 What does Rudolph Crocker leave at the Marina del Rey?
3 Who is Kit-Kat?
4 Why does Carmine help Jack?
5 Who kills Shelby?

Exercises

1 Write the correct words in your notebook.

1 astr ....*star*........... A person who works in the movies.

2 ngu   You can use this to kill someone.

3 olodb   It is red, and it is inside a person's body.

4 eifhc   The most important person in the police.

5 acklnece   You can wear this around your neck.

6 nriareg   You can wear this on your ear.

7 cifoersn   A person who looks for DNA is a

                     .... expert.

CHAPTER FOUR

2 Complete these sentences in your notebook, using the words from the box.

cable	gloves	bag	messages	van
	walk	park	nose	

1 Scylla bought some ....*gloves*........... and some electric cable.

2 Marguerite was going for a ....

3 Scylla wrote text .... to Marguerite.

4 Scylla pulled a .... over Marguerite's head from behind.

5 Scylla and Morbid threw Marguerite into the ....

6 Steemcleena stopped the van in a ....

7 Marguerite's hand flew out and hit Scylla on the ....

CHAPTER FIVE

3 In your notebook, match the correct words to the meanings.

Example: 1—g

1 They work for the police.
2 Women often carry one of these.
3 Something on your foot.
4 An open place outside an apartment.
5 A small computer.
6 Writing on a phone.
7 The killers drive it.
8 You wear this around your neck.

a terrace
b van
c shoe
d necklace
e handbag
f laptop
g officers
h message

CHAPTER SEVEN

4 Write the correct prepositions in your notebook.

1 Sci lived ....*in*.......... an old apartment.
2 Sci talked .... his friend Kit-Kat.
3 Sci's friend Darren was .... India.
4 Sci looked .... the internet.
5 A man fell .... a terrace.
6 Sci and Jack met .... Tuesday morning.
7 Jack and Sci met Nora .... the apartment building.
8 Steemcleena is working .... a group.

CHAPTER NINE

5 **Who says these words? Write the correct names in your notebook.**

Bo

Carmine

Jack

1 "Andy isn't a killer." ....*Jack*............
2 "We'll fly to Las Vegas."
3 "You helped me, and I'll help you."
4 "Who was the killer, do you know?"
5 "I'll call you when I know."
6 "What do you want?"
7 "Who paid for that?"
8 "I don't know any women in Bluffs."

CHAPTER ELEVEN

6 **Match the two parts of the sentences in your notebook.**
Example: 1—c

1 I couldn't get DNA	**a**	but he wasn't there.
2 He's sending her text messages	**b**	and hit him in the stomach.
3 They drove fast to his apartment,	**c**	from Crocker's glass.
4 We're looking for a new,	**d**	near the supermarket.
5 Graciella was in the street	**e**	and she pulled it.
6 Jack ran across the street	**f**	from a friend, Lulu.
7 Crocker was sitting	**g**	dark blue Toyota van.
8 The light was on a string,	**h**	with his hands on his head.

7 Choose the correct question word. Then, answer the questions in your notebook.

What	Where	Who	Why

1 ....*What*.......... color was the killers' van? ......*dark blue*........
2 .... couldn't they get Crocker's DNA from the glass? ....
3 .... wants to kill Graciella? ....
4 .... in Glendale does Morbid want to meet Graciella? ....
5 .... did Justine break the van window with? ....
6 .... did Jack put in a bag? ....
7 .... called Jack early in the morning? ....
8 .... did Jack throw his phone out of the window? ....

Project work

1 Write a newspaper report about pages 51–54 of the story. In your report, write about:
• where Morbid talked to Graciella
• what Jack did to Morbid
• where Justine found Crocker and what she did
• what Justine found at Crocker's apartment.
2 Find information about Los Angeles or Las Vegas. Write which state it's in, its population, its highest building, and its other important buildings.

An answer key for all questions and exercises can be found at **www.penguinreaders.co.uk**

Glossary

ago (adv.)
before now

another (det.)
a different thing or person

bar (n.)
A *bar* is a place. You can buy drinks or food and sit in it.

blood (n.)
Blood goes around your body and comes out if you cut your body. *Blood* is red.

call (v. and n.)
You *call* someone with a telephone. You make a *call*.

chief of police (n.)
a very important policeman or policewoman. The *chief of police* can tell other police *officers* to do things.

company (n.)
People work for a *company*.

dead (adj.)
not living

DNA (n.)
DNA is in all living things. It tells us about what each person, animal or plant is like.

earring (n.)
You wear an *earring* on your ear. It is a very small thing and often looks pretty.

electric cable (n.)
An *electric cable* is very long and thin and has plastic on it. It carries electricity into buildings.

expert (n.)
An *expert* knows a lot about something.

fall (v.)
to go down quickly towards the ground

forensic (adj.)
using science to find answers about crimes

gloves (n.)
You wear *gloves* on your fingers and hands.

gun (n.)
A *gun* is a machine. You point it at someone with your hand and it can hurt or kill them with bullets (= small pieces of metal).

movie star (n.)
a famous actor in a film

neck (n.)
the part of your body between
your head and shoulders
(= where your arms meet
your body)

necklace (n.)
You wear a *necklace* around your
neck. It often looks pretty.

officer (n.)
A police *officer* does important
work for the police.

professional (n.)
A *professional* is very good at
doing something and gets
money for doing it.

program (n.)
A *program* is in a computer.
It is a group of special words
and numbers.

shoot (v.)
to use a *gun* because you want
to hurt or kill someone

star (n.)
a shape (= a thing like a circle or
square) with five or more points

string (n.)
A very thin, long piece of
something. You can hold it in
your hand and pull it.

terrace (n.)
a flat place outside a house.
People sometimes sit or eat
there.

text message (n.)
a short message to someone.
You send it on a cell phone.

throw (v.)
to move your arm quickly and
push something or someone
into the air

trust (v.)
to think that someone is good
and what they say is true

van (n.)
a big car. You use it for carrying
things to different places.

win (v.)
to be the best or first in a game

Penguin 🐧 **Readers**

Visit **www.penguinreaders.co.uk**
for FREE Penguin Readers resources
and digital and audio versions of this book.